With Pugs

J. Andrew Thomas

Copyright © 2017 J. Andrew Thomas
All rights reserved.
ISBN: 1547079738
ISBN-13: 978-1547079735

By J. Andrew Thomas

available at jandrewthomas.com

Suburban Purgatory Hell

Mauled by Death in the Hot Rain

Staring into the Void of Destruction

College is for Losers (Novel)

The Garden Gnomes are Watching

Sometimes You Get Lucky and the Problem Fixes Itself

Poems for Another Day

Cattle Prod (Novel)

All My Friends are on Television

Swallow God Swallow Nothing

To my mother

who was always there for her

With Pugs

first bath

she was so small
I could have
bathed her in sink
but
it was a nice day
so I went
for the hose

I had to start off right
she was going to
be tough

no fancy
warm water
for her

like a gremlin
she hated that
water
crying and
whimpering
trying to
run away
the whole time

by the end
she looked like
a wet muskrat
terrified at what
happened

she didn't like me much
the rest of that day

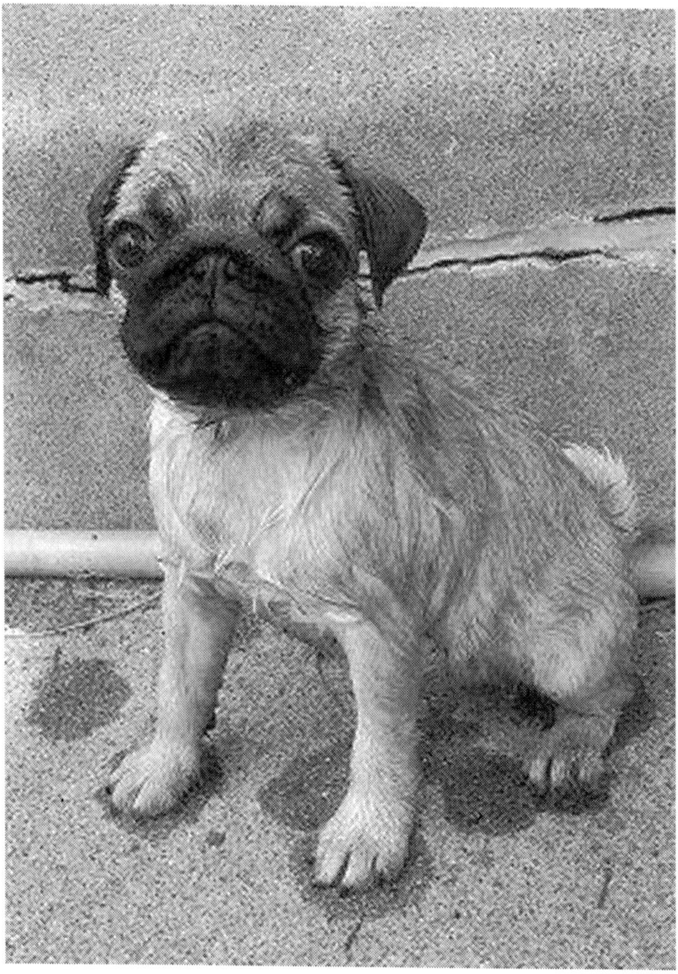

those ears

black
soft
as velvet
a perfect
contrast
to her
fawn
coat
I play with them
as she sits
in my lap
she
doesn't seem to
mind

After a month, my pug was the greatest dog ever. I loved her more than anything. She was house broken, full of energy, and slept in my bed every night. But the hair, oh god, the hair. It was the middle of the summer and she was shedding like crazy. You would pet her and then get a hand full of white bristles. It was all over the couches, the floor, and my bedsheets. I was told about it but I didn't think it would be so bad. It was the price to pay for having a cool dog. Oh well. Then, I had a conversation at work that changed it all.

"Bridget said you have two pugs," I said to Mandy.
"Yes, they are so special. When I get home they freak out and run around for at least a half an hour, screaming and crying," Mandy said.
"They are great dogs, but the shedding is horrible," I said to my co-worker.
"Oh, I know. I shave them a few times a year," she said.
"What? I thought you couldn't do that since they have a double coat."
"Nah, that's non-sense, it's fine. I can see how much cooler they are too."

She was right. It was the best piece of advice I had ever been given about dogs. 12 years later, and I'm still shaving her twice a year. Eventually, she stopped shedding all together, even when her hair grew back.

Ϋ

every day,
at the same time, I leave for work and
she knows
oh
she knows
I won't be home for eight long hours
and
she gets anxious and upset
as I pack my bag

circling around
the kitchen
barking
crying
making me feel like I am going away
forever.

I grab a treat
and throw it in the other room
and

run out the door
hoping
she will forget that I left
and will go to sleep
until I get back.

Ϋ

dirt trap

the grundle
is what I call
it

the wrinkle
in the middle
of a pug's face

you should wipe it out
every
two or three
days,
but
sometimes I get lazy
and
after a week
it's a big big mess in there.

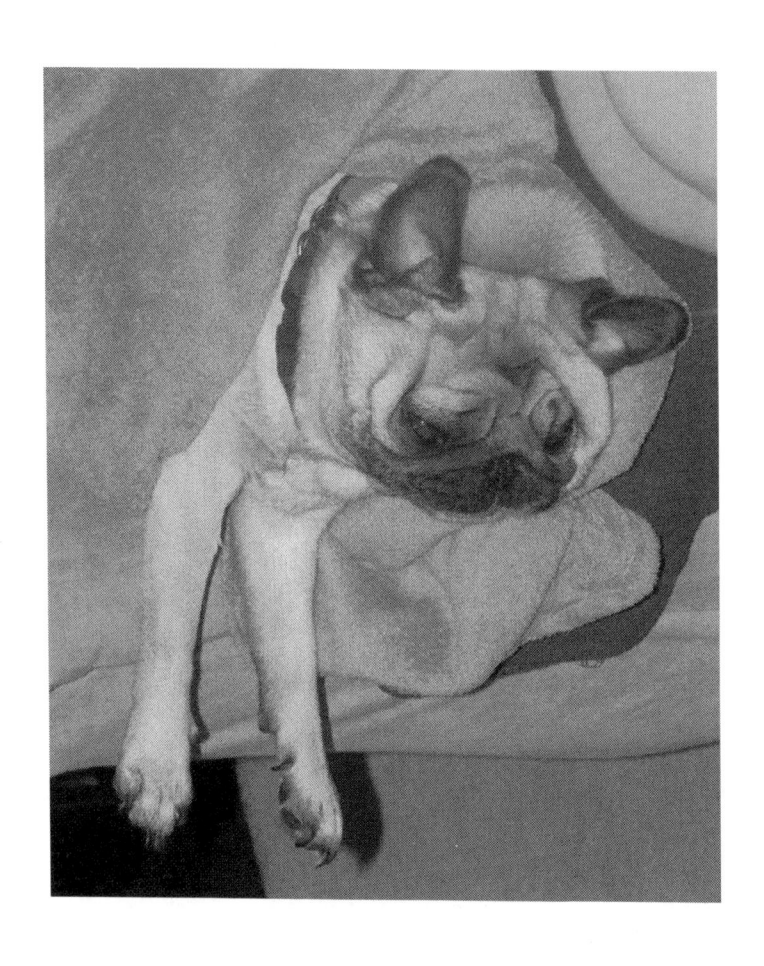

as a pug gets older
her neck fat grows and grows
like a lion's mane
it's a whole different
being

I love grabbing that big piece of
hairy skin
like pizza dough

they don't care

I feel like one of the three stooges

I look at it and it reminds me of a
Christmas wreath
on a doorway

it just showed up one day

I love it.

I first saw a Pug when I was in a veterinary office. I was 21 years old and almost finished college. I was excited to graduate and start my life. A life that would eventually involve a dog of my own. I never had my own dog. It was always "the family dog."

There were a bunch of them that I couldn't remember because I was so young. Then came Marley, a half lhasa apso, half poodle breed. Marley, like the dog in the famous book, was amazing. I loved that dog so much. But when I went off to college, I didn't see Marley that much. He became my parents dog. So, when I finished college, I wanted my own dog. A dog of my choosing.

As I sat in the vet's office with my mother and Marley (it was summer time), I looked around at all the sick dogs. German Shepard, Beagle, Terrier, and some random cats. They all seemed so normal. I always like Bulldogs, I thought. Maybe a bulldog. They had a chart of all the dog breeds in the waiting area, so I went up and checked them out. Again, I didn't see anything I liked. Then, I saw the Pug. What the hell is that? It looks like a bulldog, but not as fat and had a more smashed in face. It looks so strange, kind of like a monkey head on a dog body. I didn't know anything about them, but I knew I wanted one.

Ϋ

as the moths rose up to the light
fluttering about
like a flying
seizure patient
the world was sleeping,
and I typed away
with nobody watching except
the old sleepy pug
from her soft smelly
bed

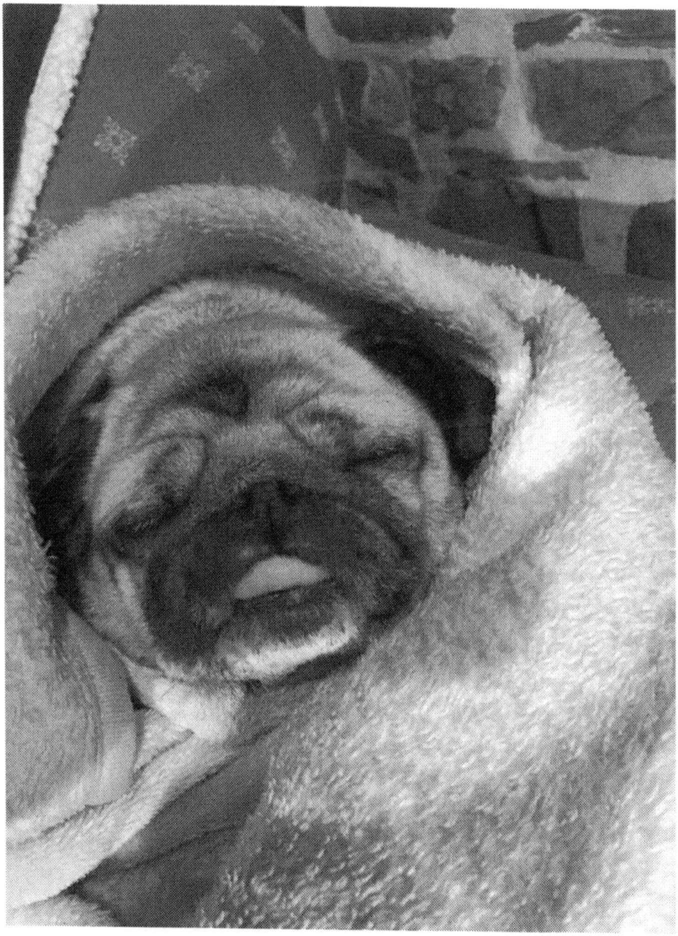

Pugs were bred for Chinese kings a long time ago. Unlike normal dogs, they were created to do *nothing*. They were only meant to be for companionship. That's what I tell people when they ask if my dog does any tricks or if she fetches.
"Nope, she just eats and sleeps and runs around aimlessly."

"Do you take her for walks?" they will then ask.

"Nope. She can walk about 100 feet and then gets hot or tired or both. Then you have to carry them."

So, when you see a lazy fat pug begging for food and sleeping on the couch, realize they are doing what they are destined to do. It's like a lion killing a zebra, that is what their instinct is. They don't even care much for other dogs, they will always go to people because people have food. Dogs offer nothing for them.
As for their flat faces, my theory is that they were trying to make them look like monkeys, which look like people. "But why are they so dumb?" I sometimes I get asked. "If they were bred for kings, shouldn't they be smarter?"
"No. Why would they? The people in power don't want anybody smarter than them. Dogs included. The dumber they were, the smarter the rulers seemed," was what I answered.

I have no clue if that is correct. All I care is that it sounds smart. It sounds right. I could have made it all up and you wouldn't have known.

Ϋ

      pick up a pug
after they eat
and
squeeze them
and
usually they
will let out a loud
      sputtering sound
like a car is back firing.

gassy gassy dogs
      they are.

a pug has a naturally grumpy
resting face
with its mouth
in a big frown.

and then
they pant
and we assume
they are happy
because that long thick tongue is out
and they smile for a bit.

☿

they sell life vests for dogs

they will try to stay afloat
for a few seconds
paddling ferociously
as their face fills
with terror and fright
but
try as they might
like a stone
dropped in a body of water
they will sink
immediately

"she always sleeps with one arm
out,

it's funny.

why does she do that?" she asked.

"I have no idea.

it's funny,
I never noticed that until
you said something but she always
does that," I said.

"I know, I have never seen a dog
sleep like that before," she said.

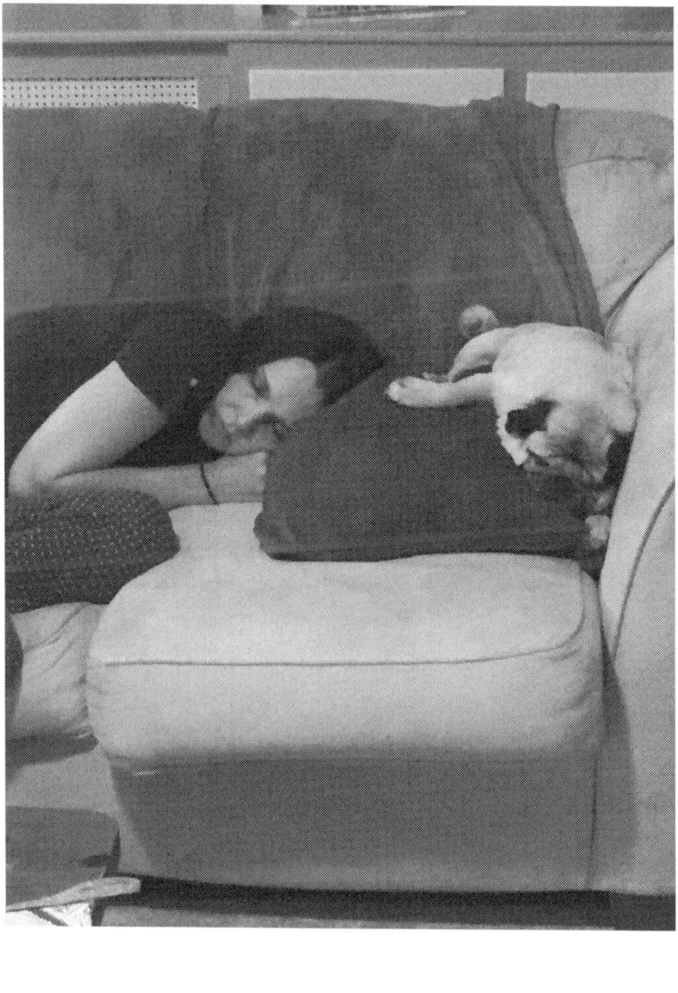

Ϋ

I have been watching her pant for an hour now wondering when it will end. She stops for 3 seconds when there is a noise or I start to get up from the couch and then it starts again. She needs air conditioning as soon as possible. If she was abandoned in the wild
she wouldn't make it very long. Maybe an hour. Luckily, she is cute, so somebody would see her wandering around and take her in immediately and she would be fine.

☥

Food is God with pugs. That is all they know.
Food. Like a homeless person, they will beg and
follow you around until you give in. It's all they
think about.

☥

As I sit here at 3 in the morning, churning out page
after page of my stupid novel, it's comforting to see
her there, sleeping like the world is ok for a minute.

nothing phases her. and there I was writing all the
ills of the our existence
hoping things would get better
not realizing
things were just fine
where I was at.

please stop

we don't like it
when they
fight
it's loud and angry and
scary
we bark and bark
at them
to stop
but
they don't. it just makes them
yell louder. so we will hide
until it's safe to come
out.

𐂂

I remember the first day I brought her home. I decided that Zooey was her name. After the famous actress who had been named after the Salinger book. I had an evil cat named Ozzy, after the singer, who would swipe and bite at you if you crossed her. A real wild one, almost feral. She was always like that. A farm cat from the beginning, she couldn't be tamed.

I really didn't want to get her declawed, I had read that it was such a barbaric act to help save your couches. But, I knew she wouldn't put up with a "stupid" dog. In cat's eyes, all dogs are morons. So, a few weeks before, I took her to the vet, and got it done. I felt terrible when she could barely walk in her bandages. Did I make a bad decision? What else was I to do?

When I plopped a 9 week old Zooey on the kitchen floor, she ran all around the house, exploring her new home. She kept circling the TV room over and over. "What is she doing?" my wife asked with a confused look on her face.

"This is what they do," I said.

I looked around for the cat and she was nowhere to be found. Anytime there was a new visitor in the house, she would hide.

An hour later, Ozzy, came up from the basement and skulked around in a corner, peering at her new roommate. Zooey didn't even see her, she was oblivious, sitting there panting from her non-stop running.

I pointed to the cat and said "This should be interesting."
A few minutes later, the cat silently walked up to Zooey, and stared at her from about 6 inches away. Ozzy had a mean look on her face, like *What the hell are you doing here? This is my house.*
Ozzy raised her paw slowly towards Zooey's head and she stopped panting and looked scared. I could see her whiskers trembling with fear.
Whap! Whap! Whap!
Like a rapid fire machine gun
3 smacks right to Zooey's face.
I launched off the couched and shooed the cat away. I grabbed Zooey and held her tight. Ozzy fled back downstairs.
She was disabled, her dangerous claws were no more. The mighty feline had been beaten and Zooey would be safe from then on.

they don't judge
no matter
how fat
how stupid
how drunk
or
poor
you are

all that matters is
you are there

that's it

show up
and you get
pure love

as long as they
get food
and a warm lap

gods,
godly dogs
they are

☂

is this it?

I come in at night
after work
and she's
sleeping
dead as a doornail
barely breathing

I throw down my keys
on the table
hoping

she will hear
but

she doesn't move at all

oh no
is this it?

I pry off my shoe
and touch her head
with my socked foot

she moves a little
like she has arisen
from a 10 year slumber
with a look on her face
like
what do you want?

I tap her again
and she springs up
remembering
it's time
to eat

I give her food,
let her out
and
10 minutes later
she is on the couch
belly full of food

soft pillow
snoring away.

Ϋ

Pugs are accessory dogs. They don't work well by themselves, like a Golden Retriever or a Lab or lots of other dogs. You either have two or more of them in a house, which will result in complete idiocy and delight or you can bundle a pug with another dog. Any dog is fine, they will get along with whatever you pair them with. This is because the pug will not try and dominate the other dog. Thus, the other dog will become the alpha by default and will protect the pug.

with dogs

there is the <u>tail up</u>
and
the <u>tail down</u>

but the pug
has the middle tail
when it is unsure
about
the situation

it's rare
but
you can
photograph it
if you are
ready.

chainsaw em' down

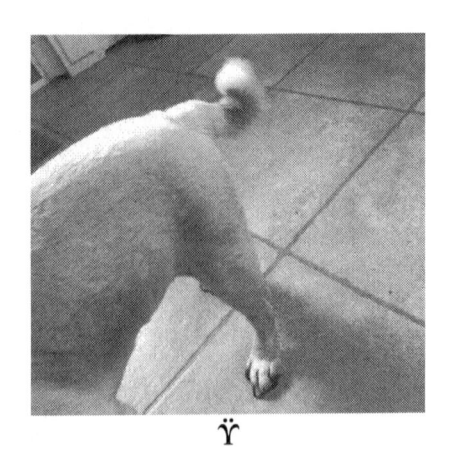

her nails
are getting so damn
long

like
wolverine's claws

I want to cut them
but the struggle
will be much

too much

I need half a day
to get them down

black like coal

they are hard to
chop
as I will always
get one bleeder

tomorrow…maybe
or the next day
or the next

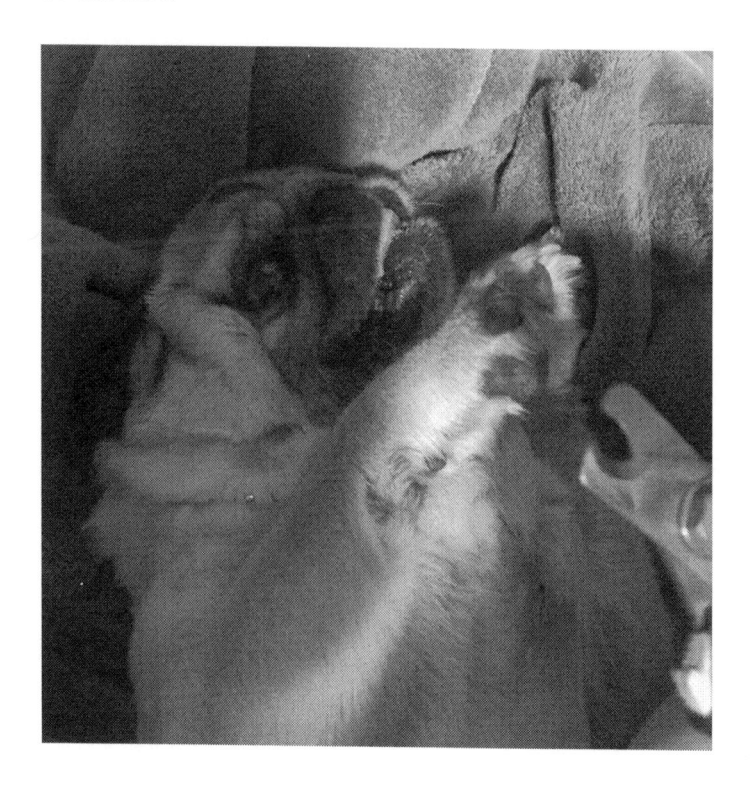

the car can be
an anxious place
for a pug

they don't care
where they are going
it only matters
how fast

on the way to
wherever you're going
full of pep
endless energy
from sleeping for 10 hours

they don't bark or cry
they scream
 a high shrilled noise
that I have never heard
anywhere else
weeeeeOOOOAAARRRR!!!

like they are
constipated and
angry and
nervous

they run back and forth to each window
making mucus marks
on the glass

with their wet noses

they jump up
on the arm rest
and put their paw onto a button

the automatic window
comes down
half way

fresh air!

freedom!

you look back and yell at them
and put the window up
and then
hit the "lockout" key

the screaming continues
followed by
a lunge into the front seat

"hey! get back there!" as you
grab them by the scruff
and place them in the back seat
at a red light.

Finally,
you arrive
it's only been

7 minutes
but it feels like an hour.

as you leave the car
you can see their eyes
bulge out even more
and a frantic
long yell comes at you
through the window.

you pretend to walk away

because it's fun to tease for a moment

and then

you come back
and lead them to their destination.

☥

My favorite scene in Rocky II is when Rocky goes to Mickey's run-down apartment to ask him to train him again for another title fight against Apollo Creed and then Mickey tries to talk him out of it, saying he will get beaten badly. He tells Rocky that he can't see out of his right eye and shows him by slapping him in the head and then says

"Now you didn't even see that comin', did ya? And that's comin' from a broken down pug like me. What... what do ya think the champ would do to ya?"

☥

I like her Buddha belly
when she sits under my arm
with me
I poke that soft skin
and it makes me happy.

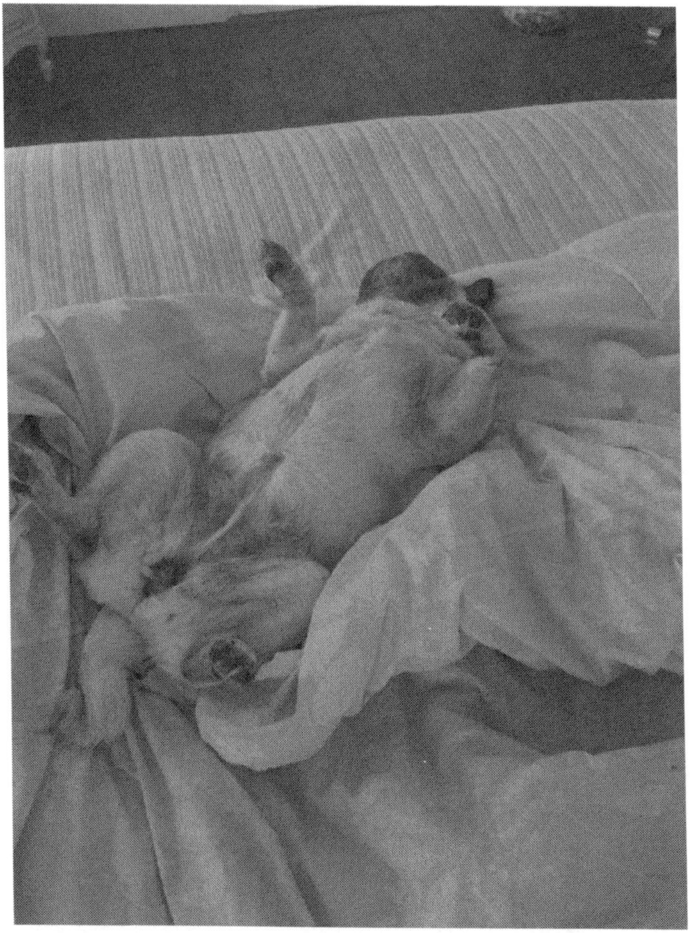

☥

She seemed fine without a leash. She was so tiny. I knew that small dogs would chase anything they saw and not listen when you called them. But I thought if that happened, I would be able to catch her if that happened. Besides, she liked being off the leash, running around the soft green summer grass. I should have been smarter, more cautious. I lived on a busy street where cars would barrel home in rush hour. Many cats died in front of my house. That is why I never let Ozzy out of the house, it was simply too dangerous. But Zooey was fine. She was only 11 weeks, the size of a small bunny rabbit. She was running around the house like a nut but outside she would just lay around and chill.

I don't know what she saw that day but it was something worth running after. I think it was some strange man walking to the store down the street. Many people who worked there would walk down that busy street to their job. Well, when she saw that dude, she took off with lightning speed. I had never seen her run so fast in a straight line. Right toward the road. My blood went cold. I didn't even have time to start
Running. She was in the middle of the street. A giant delivery truck slammed on its

breaks as I watch little Zooey freeze with fear at the giant machine in front of her. I ran out and grabbed her and told the driver "Thank you, Thank you, Thank you!" He looked stunned himself that he was able to react so fast. I could feel Zooey shaking with terror.

That was her one and only free pass. Never again did I let her roam free like that.

☥

many many many
nights
alone
I sat there
with nobody
except a pug
and the television

people asked what I was doing
with myself
if I needed any
help

"No!"
I screamed.

and it was like that
for a long time

but I wasn't just sitting there
I was waiting

waiting for the tide to turn

waiting for the sun to come out
for
things to change
finally.

they did
and slowly
I came out
clawed my way back to
humanity
to
society
alone
by myself
with the dog by my side.

I wouldn't have had it
any other way.

Ϋ

they look at you
from across
the room
sometimes
staying afar
because
the closer
they get
the
better the chance
they will be trapped
in a couch
black hole.

Those big bulgy lovable eyes; always full of worry and hope.

Ϋ

I have found that people who own pugs are
generally a little askew themselves,
myself
included.

walking

I am glad I have a dog
she is an old pug
11 going on 12 years
been with me since the beginning.

I used to walk her
everyday
she had too much energy
had to run her out

it's not acceptable
for a man to
walk alone
in the park.

I see them
these loner guys
with their hands in the pockets
unwashed hair
rags for clothes
looking like death is near.

they look like serial rapists
but a man with a dog
looks perfectly fine.

the bored housewives,
energetic, hopeful 20 year olds
all came up, squealed with excitement
and pet the pug.

a man can either run alone
or walk a dog
there is no other way.

now,
my old dog can't make it
on those hot days
so I bought an old
red wagon.

I put a blanket in there
for the dog.
I pull her around
and the looks I get
are priceless

they must think
I am insane
pulling this
broken down
old pug
in a
red wagon.

better than
walking alone.

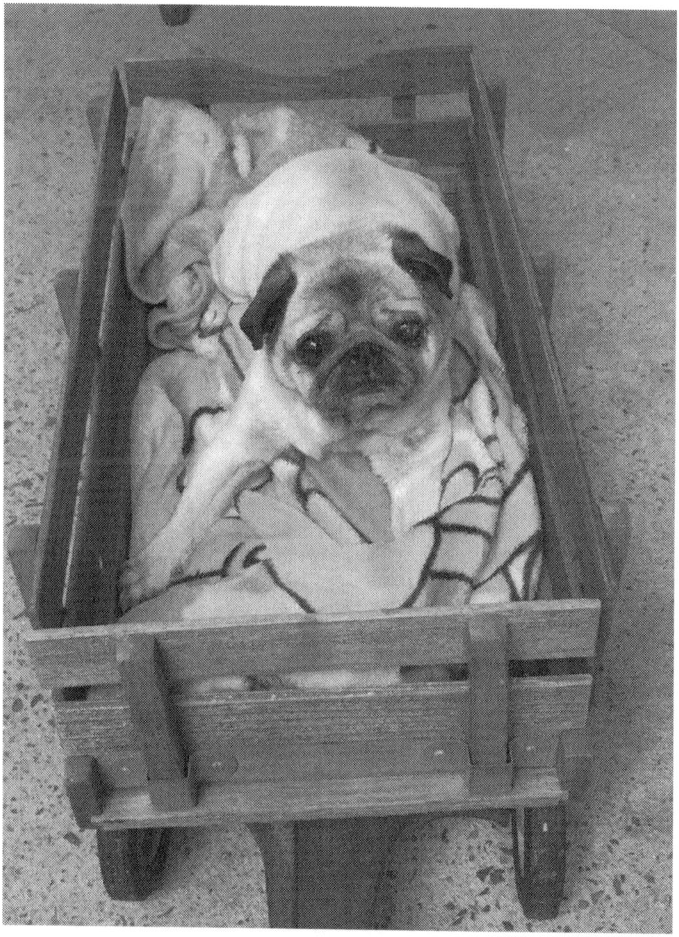

̈Ϋ

I have a drawer in my house filled with birthday cards with all different depictions of pugs on them. Some are photos, some are drawings, all are supposed to be "wacky." Once you get a pug, people will associate you with them forever. I should throw them out but I like looking at them from time to time. Some of them are truly bizarre and make me feel good for a split second. I think, *my dog could be on one of those cards*. She is such a clown sometimes, I just need to keep my camera ready for that perfect picture.

̈Ϋ

7 more years

"I ran into a really
cute girl today
with an 18 year old
pug." he said.

"are you serious?" I said.

"yea, she had dark
curly hair, cute."

"the pug was 18?"

"yes, and blind as a bat."

"oh man, so I have
7 more years with
this dog?"

"haha, that is what
I was thinking."

"I don't even know
if I have 5 more years
in me."

"I know, right."

"did you get her number?"

"nah, not yet. maybe next
time. she is probably dating
some crazy person."

"100% chance"

"yup"

we dress them up
and they look more ridiculous
if
that's even
possible

it's too bad
they will never
realize how much
joy
they bring us.

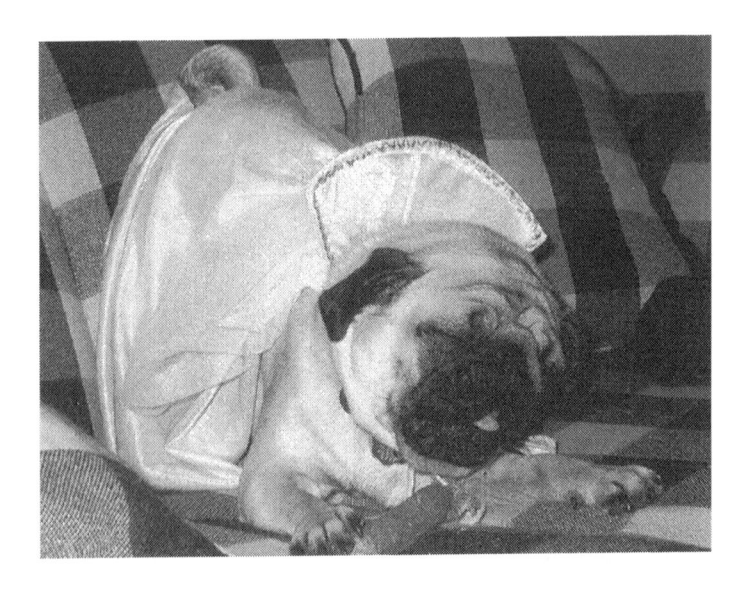

Zooey

I have had the same dog
my whole adult life
going on 12 years.

this old pug
sleeps beside me
every night.

she is looking
haggard
but still kicking.

I wonder
what it will be like
when she is gone.

she's been through it all
seen everything.

just waking up
and not seeing her
wagging her tail
waiting
for food
and then
to be let out.

it will definitely be weird.

she could go to 15
who knows?

bananas

my favorite activity
during the
mid afternoon
while I sit around
and wait to go
into work
is feeding pieces
of banana
to my overzealous
pug.

she will sit on the red
soft pillow
on my couch
as the banana
(fully peeled)
sits on my
chest
as I pound the keys.

every few minutes
I take a piece off
and pop it in my
mouth
and then I share
a smaller

piece
with her.

she is patient
most of the time
but
occasionally
she will
try and lick
the banana
on my
shirt.

when it's all gone
she will become
disinterested
with me
and jump onto the floor
and to her
bed
where she waits
for my next
snack.

Ϋ

like a magnet
to a piece of metal
they will stick to you
non-stop

whenever they get close

Ϋ

the snoring

lying dog
down on the pillow
she
doesn't care about anything

dead asleep
for some reason
nobody knows
living for nothing
we all want the life
but not

don't strive for that
life
it doesn't exist
just. just. do

do your thing

just.

do your thing.

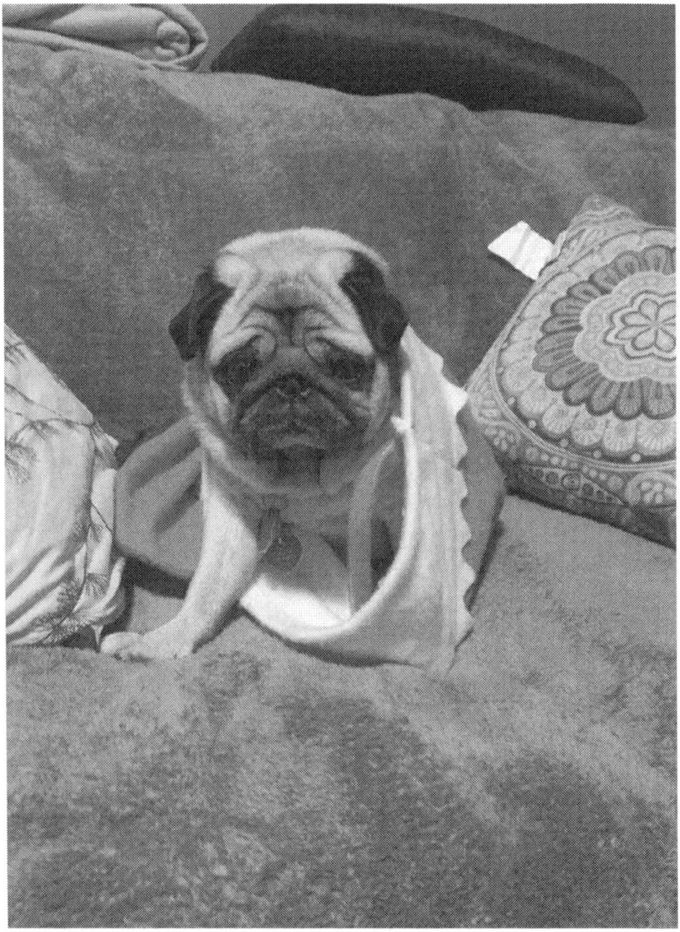

Ϋ

Dogs have saved more lives than doctors have

(I have proof).

mini me

it's like
we designed them
to follow
our every move
like
they can't even
think for themselves

dogs
yes
dogs
are so domesticated
they don't
act on their own
instinct anymore.

whatever we do
they do
following us
around all day
like a personal
assistant

and
for some reason
it makes us *feel*
less alone

even though
we are.

bliss

I wish I could
get as much joy
in anything
as my dog
dragging her behind
on the rug

my wife
used to yell at
the old dog
blissfully
wiping her
old tired ass
across the
floor

not me
I let her go.

the look on
her smashed face
is delightful.

I let that girl
go.

☥

Watch out what you feed them, if they get too fat, they will look like walking D-Cell batteries.

☥

we all

want to live in the present
not thinking about
the past
or the
future

yet

pugs do that naturally
how is that possible?

they have 30 second
memories
and we call them
dumb
which seems ridiculous.

☥

she sleeps more and more
like an old lady
who
doesn't want any
part of the world

I marvel at the hours she logs

12 years old now
still going strong

the median age for pugs
is
11

she looks good
still eating
gets up in the morning
all excited
to go out

she might make it past 100

I sure hope so

☥

"What type of dog will you get next?" she asked.

"Hmmmm," I said.

I thought about it for a moment and realized that I didn't want to live in the world without a pug.

I decided at that moment I would always have a pug if it was feasible.

"I would like to get a Corgi but only if I have a pug as well," I said. "I miss having two dogs."

"Those are weird too."

"Perfect."

Ϋ

when they are young
they will guard you
obsessively
barking at
everything in site…

…but only to a
point

and then
will
give up
entirely

for
a nap.

Ϋ

Pugs are known as the "clowns" of dogs
but they aren't scary
like the ones at the circus

☥

I don't trust these guys

I took my dog to the
vet
yesterday

her eye was constantly
filled with green
goop

I cleaned it daily
for 4 weeks
and it never
got better

I was going to keep
letting it go
but a woman
pushed me into
the dog doctor's office.

in that small room
my dog and I waited
10 minutes
and when the doctor finally
arrived
he looked at the dog
for 5 minutes
and said she had

"dry eye"
and prescribed
some drops

10 minutes later
I got a bill
for 170.23

Holy Crap, I thought.

how can this be?

5 minutes and some
medicine. 170 dollars please.

yet,
I hear people saying that
we need to rescue
as many dogs as we can

who can afford it? these
crooks are preying on
people
who love animals.

they know we are closer to
our pets than
our kids and jack up
the costs
year after year.

rescue a dog, rescue a dog!

I would have 10 of them
if I could

but I can't
because when things go bad
which they always do
I won't be able to
afford rent.

Ϋ

We will achieve world peace when the earth is filled
with happy
pugs clumsily running around
bumping into
each other
not judging anybody.

packs

most animals in their groups
of more than
three
have vocabulary terms
to describe them

a gaggle of geese
a pack of gorillas
a herd of sheep
a mob of kangaroos
a school of fish

and somebody came up
with the name
for a group of pugs

it's called a "grumble"

which is a perfect name
but

there is really no reason
for this term
as
a naturally occurring pack
of pugs
would never occur

in the wild.

I see those eyes

crazy eyes

when I open the refrigerator door
looking
for whatever
she can get

she stands there
both front feet on the shelf
looking up
tail wagging
tongue flapping
looking at me

hoping I get something tasty
this time.

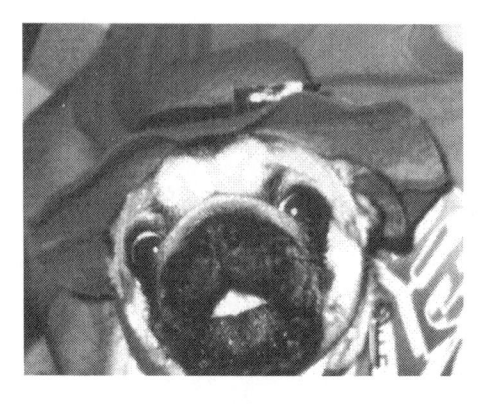

♈

    I saw an article
about what dog you should own
according to your
astrological sign.

I don't know why but I always clicked
on dumb stuff like that.

it was because the internet was tracking me
no
tracking US

it knew what I wanted
and put it front of my face

dogs, beer, video games,
movies
television
cars
books

that's what I looked at
and
that is what popped up
on a daily
basis

so

as I scrolled through
to the end
where the fish sign was

I was shocked when it said

PISCES – PUGS
People born under this sign are highly sensitive and seek attention from their loved ones. Playful and childlike, Pugs too need constant companions and will be the ideal choice for Pisceans.

it still didn't make me believe my horoscope
but I did agree
with what it said

pugs over people
that's for
sure

ϓ

no clue

as the world was burning to the ground
on a daily basis
and everyone was
fearing for their lives

and all she did was stare at me
waiting for the next
move
the next
meal
the next
car trip

and I was jealous
that she didn't know anything
that was going on
nor did she
care.

viral video

if you
got online
you could find endless
almost
infinite
wacky YouTube videos
on pugs
but
I think my favorite
is the one
where
the pug
spins around
every time
the blender is
turned on. it's like
it has no control over
itself

I tried it on my dog
hoping
it would work
but sadly
it didn't.

Ϋ

You talk to them as if you were talking to a person
and then they tilt their heads
like they are trying to understand
what you are saying

sometimes I just
babble
non-sense at them
just
to see them
try
and figure out what
I am trying
to
convey.

ϔ

that black snout and closed eyes
she can't stop panting

it's 97 degrees today
   relentless
humid
heat
that is microwaving
all of us

I turn the
air conditioning on her
full blast
   hoping
she will cool off
but it's not
working

like an old car
with a bad radiator
all pugs
will get over heated
in 5 short minutes
and then it will take a few hours
trying to get them
to cool off.

watching them

with that tongue out
gasping for air
just
laying on the floor
looking like
they will die

there's not much you can
do
other than
wait it out.

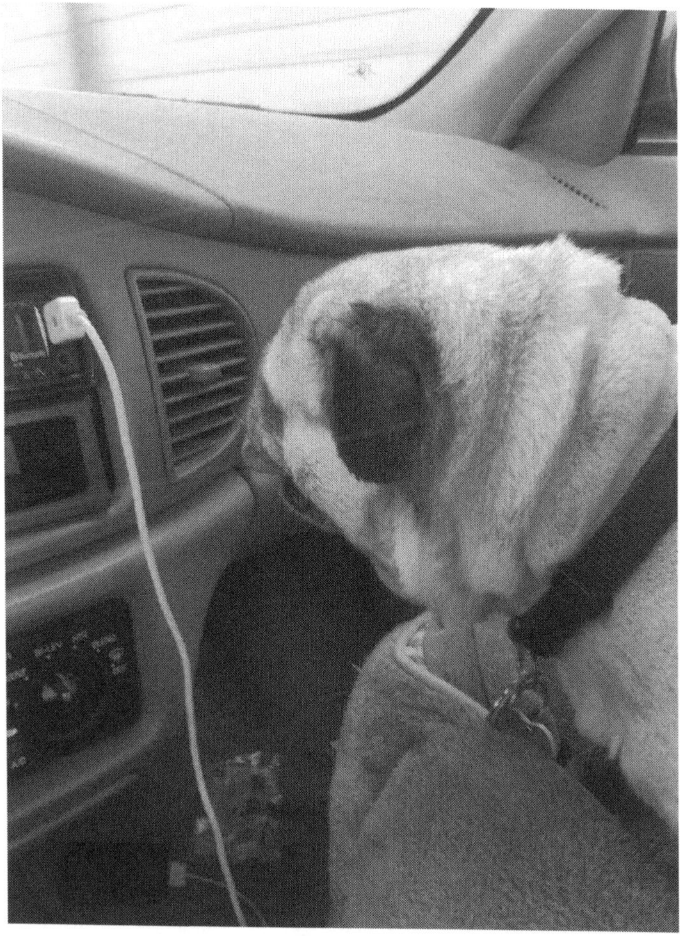

☥

her whole life I never had to take her to a strange
place. My mother would always watch her. But now,
I have no other choice.
I feel like a mother handing off her child to the
Nazi's.
Who are these people
watching my dog?
They seem nice
but
I don't trust them any more than
I trust the cashier at the grocery store.
What other choice do I have? The kennel where
she will sit alone in a cage all day and be lonely and
scared? I think it will be fine, their house is nice and
what reason
would they have to hurt my dog? Yes, it will be fine,
I know it.
but then
we get to her temporary home:

she was
housebroken for 12 years
but in that
   new house
she runs around
anxious
like a nut-job

she

sniffs around
and
pees on the rug
as she stares at
the pet sitter

I see her game
she is smart

make them not
go away

"I don't want to say here!" she
looks at me.

smart.

but the man is kind
and says

"it's expected"

and then he lures
her to the kitchen
with a tasty treat
and we sneak out
without saying "goodbye"
because I know it will be easier
that way
but
I still feel bad.

Ϋ

one in the same

I prefer fawn
pugs
over
the
black ones
but
I have heard
that the
black ones
don't
shed
which makes no
sense
at all,
but
they are all pugs
so
why should it?

Ϋ

I love all dogs. How can you not? But I look at them, all those normal hairy mammals, and think:

"Pugs are so much weirder, like me."

Ϋ

she waits
patient
silent
staring
like
nobody
I have
ever
seen

nowhere to go
except
upstairs
in
that soft
soft
bed
where
she
sleeps like
a
queen

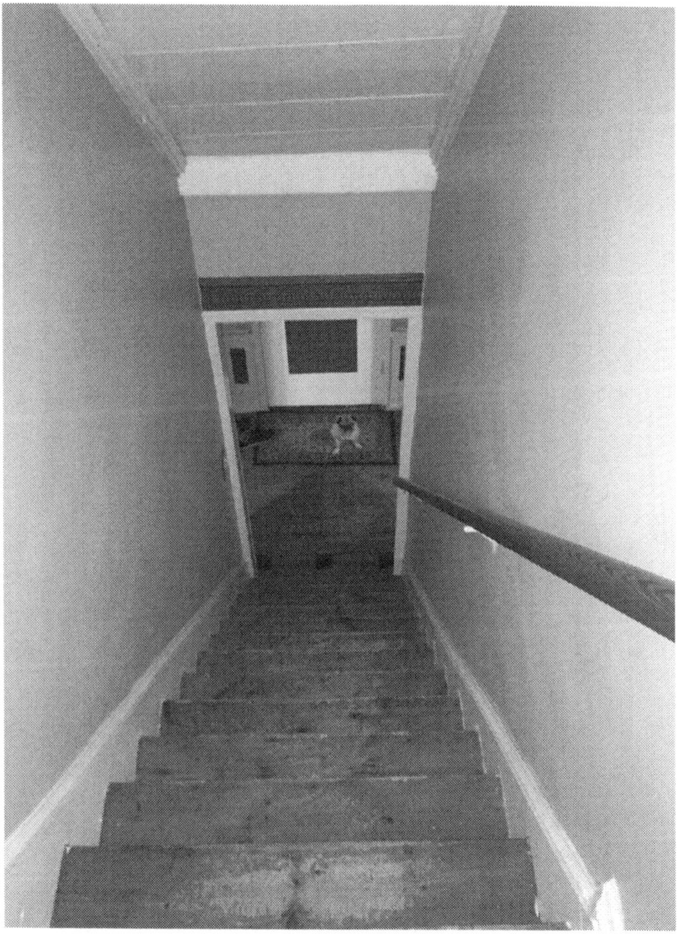

For weeks she was squatting all over the house. She couldn't stop. Red urine. UTI, I thought. Ok, so I added cranberry juice to her water. She sniffed it and wasn't having it. So I went to the cranberry pills from the pharmacy. This will fix it. 3.99 for a bottle, nice and affordable.

A week later, nothing changed. And to the vet she went.

The doctor asked his normal questions and then took her to the back room.

He came back with the X-Ray 15 minutes later and gave me the bad news:

"It's not a UTI. She has a huge bladder stone," he said as he put the plastic sheet on the lighted board.

"Holy crap!" I said.

"Yea, it's too big to try and dissolve. We need to operate."

"How much will it cost?" I asked automatically.

"It's around a thousand dollars."

It wasn't even a decision even though I was dead broke. I set the operation up and gave them my credit card. I would have to slave away late in the night for weeks to pay for it. Nothing in my life had been worth it. 5 years later as she circles the kitchen excited for her food, I would do it 10,000 more times.

Ϋ

they were best buddies
for
5 long years
sleeping together
playing
barking
running around like
nut jobs

I wonder if she remembers
Doug
her
wiener dog friend

even though dogs
don't have
short term memories
but
what about long term?

I forget things every minute
but
I remember
events from
20 years ago.

she lost her pep since he
left

doesn't get excited as much

most days she doesn't even remember
he existed

some days

she lays there
for hours
not sleeping
just
staring at the wall
morose
and
I can tell she misses him.

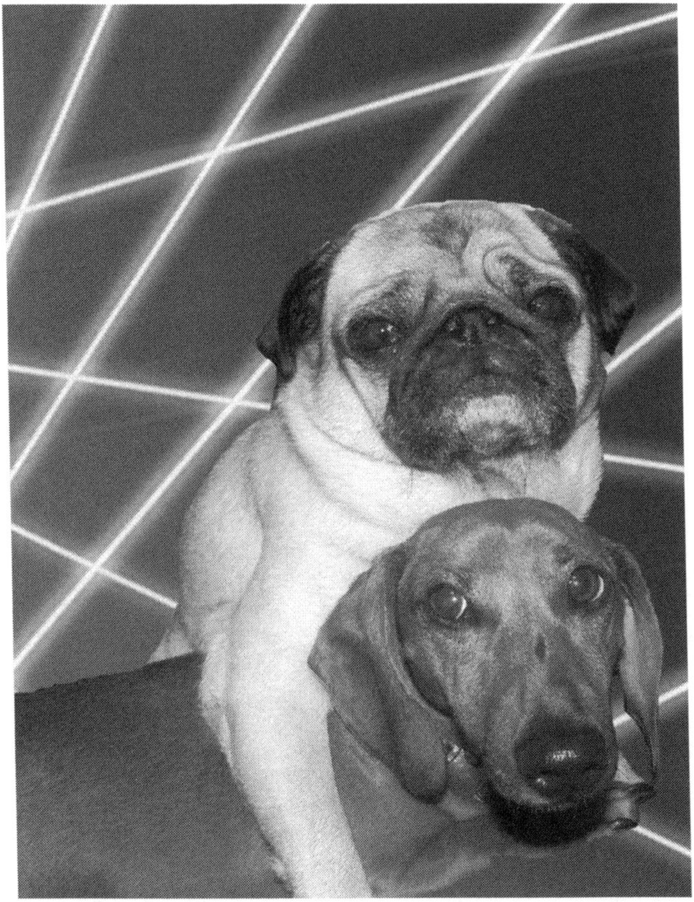

Ϋ

I took her out for a walk the same time every day. I had to go to work at 4:00, so 2:15 was the perfect time. She plodded along, panting and stopping every 50 feet, catching her breath. As we got to the end, a crazy old man got out of his car with his French bulldog and then got excited when he saw me with my pug.

I saw him on a daily basis but he seemed to forget we saw him the day before and the day before that and the day before that. I would avoid him because the first time the dogs met, the bulldog smelled Zooey for a few seconds and bit her right in the face even though she didn't do anything.. I pulled her back and then the old man laughed. I checked her face and she was bleeding from the cheek. So from now on, I keep her away even though he tries to get them to interact.

I don't know what is wrong with him. I don't know what is wrong with most people.

Ϋ

"I got a pug."

"Oh, so you got one of those alien dogs?"

"Yup, that's the one!"

Ϋ

Sitting there, not sleeping, just staring ahead at the wall. What can they be thinking?
Anything?
They look so restful, so ready to take on whatever comes their way.

☥

that first night

deserted,
abandoned,
left stranded,

in that

desolate,
empty,
godforsaken,

house…

nothing seemed right.

life was over.

what's the point?

why should I keep
going on?

then I thought of the words
of the famous
Mickey Rourke
when he was down and
out

"Yeah, I didn't want to be here, but I didn't want to kill myself. I just wanted to push a button and disappear.... I think I hadn't left the house for four or five months, and I was sitting in the closet, sleeping in the closet for some reason, and I was in a bad place, and I just remember I was thinking, 'Oh, man, if I do this,' [and] then I looked at my dog, Beau Jack, and he made a sound, like a little almost human sound. I don't have kids, the dogs became everything to me. The dog was looking at me going, 'Who's going to take care of me?'"

I looked at my pug
and
it did make sense. she was still there.

why should I
punish her
unwavering loyalty

she did nothing wrong
except
be there
day in and day out

and she is still there
to this day
at home
in her
bed
or on the couch

waiting for me
to get off
work.

☿

For weeks, the smell kept emanating from the dogs behind. A stinky horrible smell that was indescribable.

"What is that?" I asked.

"It's her anal gland, she is spraying all over the couch!" she screamed.

"Oh. What does that mean?"

"You have to take her to the vet, they can express them."

"Great, more money."

"I called, it's only 30 bucks."

Nah, I can do this on my own, I thought. That is what the internet is for. I can find out how to do anything on there.

So after a few websites and videos of people showing how to express dog anal glands, I was ready to go.

I held my pug steady as I put her butthole a few inches from my face. The people said to put both thumbs on either side of the anus and then push them at the same time. Then a stinky liquid will come dribbling out and then you wipe with a moist towel. Ok, easy enough.

I had her in place. Thumbs ready. 1,2,3, push!

Then
It happened

A brown sludge came spraying out onto my face and into my eyes

Ahhhh!

The stink!

It was all too fast. I had no chance to get out of the way. The dog went running into the other room to hide while I went and washed off my face. I went and found the dog and wiped her butt. I gave it a smell and it seemed better. It worked!

Later, when the woman came home, I told her about what happened and she laughed and laughed.
    "I can still smell it on you," she said.
    "Really?"
    "It's awful."

One shower didn't do it. It was like I was sprayed by a skunk. It took a few scrubbings to get it off for good.

30 bucks. What a deal.

ӵ

When sitting alone at the dog park, my Pug never ventures far from my feet. I don't know why I go. It's mostly for the comments people make:

> "What kind of dog is that?"
> "Oh that's the dog from Men in Black"
> "She looks hot, is she ok?"
> "Does she bite?"

And then, a strange lady with a pug or two pugs or no pugs, comes up to me with her wide eyes and crazy hair and says how much she loves "these dogs" and that we need to setup a play date for our dogs.
   "Yes," I say always.

the ritual

out there in the lawn
she sniffs
the whole yard
before finding her
spot
then
when she finds it
she circles around
over and over
and over
faster
and faster
until
blam!

when she is done
she kicks out the grass
with her back
legs
two times
always
two times

it's a ritual
buried in her
small

brain
and it makes
absolutely
no sense.

☥

How do they get so tired when all they do is eat, go outside for a few minutes and then eat again?

Sophie's choice

I had my choice: the little girl or the fat boy. The girl was scrawny and rambunctious. The boy was fat and lugubrious. He was nicknamed "Tank" because he was so slow and big. They were both cute in their own way. But I thought about the future and how much fatter the boy would get. I watched them play and the girl was running circles around the boy. He seemed winded only after a few minutes. I saw those giant pugs at the park, they could barely move. I picked up the girl and held her in my one hand. She was the size of a guinea pig. She wagged and panted. I looked into those big black globes of excitement. Yes, this is the one, I thought.

Ϋ

I remember the first time I tried to play fetch with a pug. It didn't last long. The dog excitedly ran after the tennis ball and then tried to pick it up but she couldn't fit in her mouth because her face was too flat. She then ran back to me and begged for a treat. From then on, I didn't make any attempt to teach her any tricks or walk her. I anointed her a "couch dog" from then on.

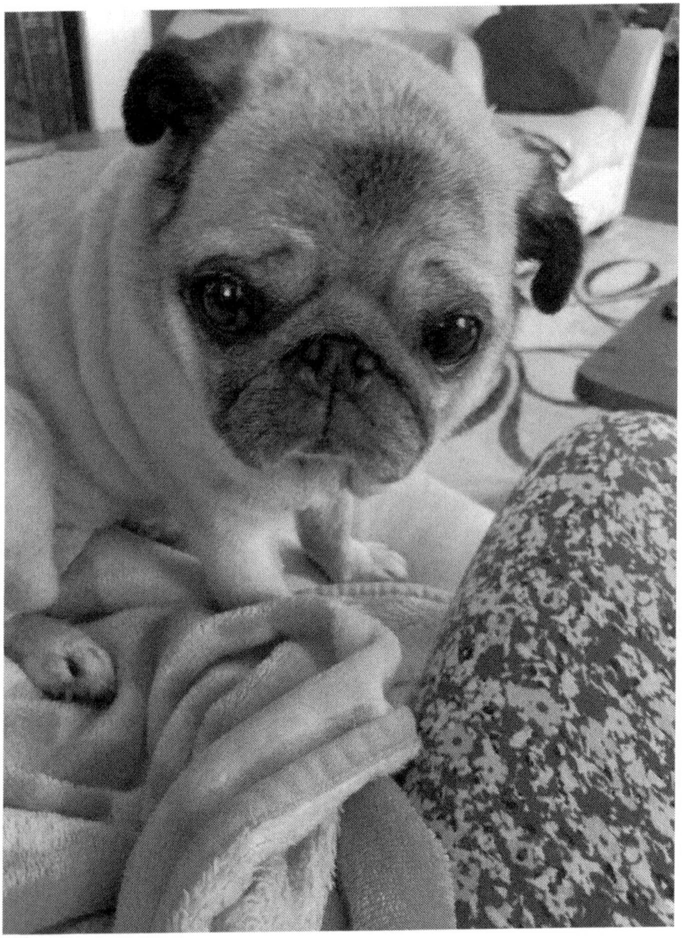

Ϋ
few people
know
that the pug has a
built in
sneeze
button

put your finger
on the nose
for
one second
and then
let go

out one will
come
sometimes
fast
and loud
sometimes
low
and quiet

no more!

under the coffee table
I will wait

it's coming
I know it

every morning the same
it's the same cooking smell
then
the banging of the dishes
followed by the
walk to the TV room
and then
    glorious
food
dropped from
    above

this is my only shot
of the day
to get some decent food
around here

that damn dog food
tastes like
garbage

over and over
the same thing
every day
for
12 years
I think I will stop eating it
soon
then maybe
I can get some of the good stuff

it's not fair
I know it
he knows it
but still
it's the same cup of dried
crap
once in the morning
once at night

no more!

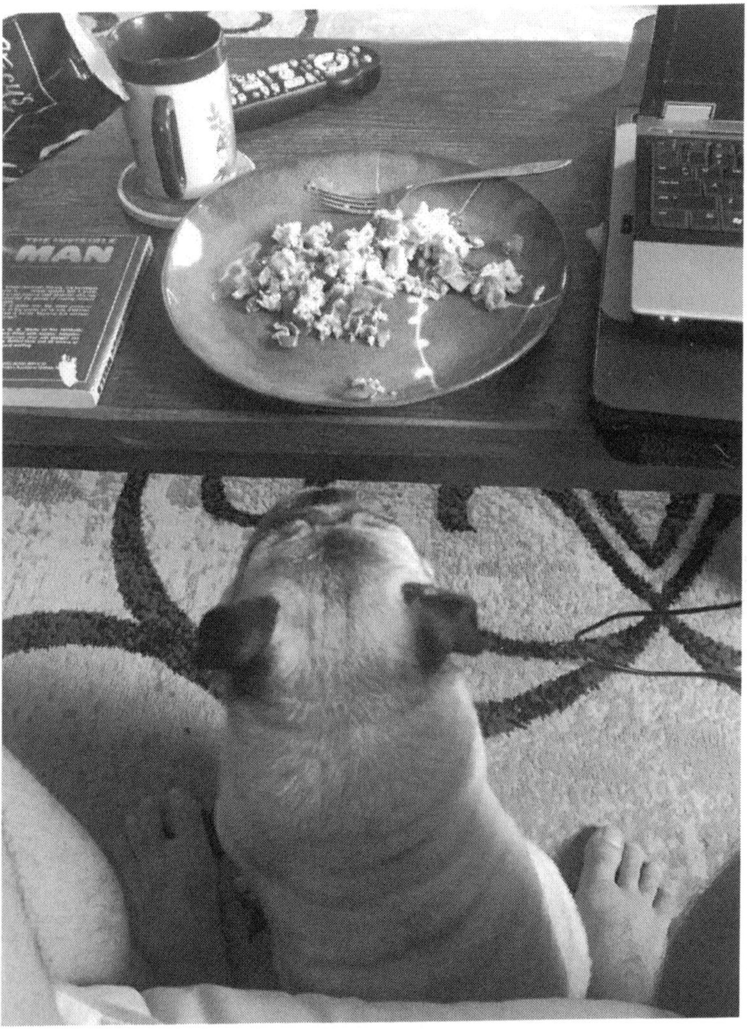
MAN

cyanide

it amazes me
that dogs don't
come with instructions
like Gizmo
from *The Gremlins* movie.

sure
we all know not to give them chocolate

but
avocados and
grapes (which can shut down
my pug's kidneys!)

who would know this?

now
whenever I am eating those
purple globes
and one
falls to the floor
panic fills my brain
and I have to quickly drop
to the
ground so my dog can't
eat the delicious fruit.

sometimes,
one will roll under
a piece of furniture and I
have to search around
    for hours
looking for it because

poison on the carpet
is dangerous
to my best friend.

Ϋ

laying there
like a loaf of bread
on the pillow

rolls and rolls
of skin
bound up
like a pack of
hotdogs
on her back

I like to grab them
and
knead them between
my fingers

like those relaxation
tools

in between
the poems
and the
television

ϔ

homebody

we get along
so well

both of us
like it in the house

sitting on the couch
eating
drinking
relaxing

the world out there
is overrated

I look at her
she looks at me
and we
laugh
at all the people
running around
like
nutjobs

looking for something they
will never
find.

when no one else is around
and your
feelin'
down

pick up a beer
then

grab your pug
like a suitcase
and
sit her down
in her
      place

right next to you
and she
will
cure your winter time
      blues.

J. Andrew Thomas is a writer of fiction and poetry and lives outside of Philadelphia with his 12 year old pug Zooey. He graduated from Kutztown University in 2003 with a degree in biology and worked in the pharmaceutical industry for 12 years before starting to write. At age 35, he wrote his first novel over a four month period and since then has authored several collections of poetry and another two novels. For more information visit the author's website: jandrewthomas.com.

Photo by Christian Aristizabal

Alexis Auman contact:

alexis.auman6@gmail.com

Portfolio:

https://alexisauman.myportfolio.com

Christian Aristizabal contact:

chrisaristizabal@hotmail.com

Zooey the Pug YouTube Channel:

https://www.youtube.com/channel/UCXoNL65T3eySZ8Jci5CtHJw

Made in the USA
Columbia, SC
09 May 2021